INDIVISIBLE

Healing Meditations

Lindsay Fleming

All Scriptures are taken from the *Holy Bible, New King James Version*. Copyright © 1982, 2013 by Holman Bible Publishers. Used by permission.

INDIVISIBLE
Copyright © 2018 Lindsay Fleming

All rights reserved. Except as permitted under the US Copyright Act of 1976, no part of this publication may be reproduced, distributed or transmitted in any form or by any means electronic or mechanical, including photocopying, recording, or any information storage/database system and retrieval system now known or to be invented, without prior permission in writing from the author, except by a reviewer who wishes to quote brief parts of the text in connection with a review written for inclusion in a source of media.

Cover Design/Interior Design: Lindsay Fleming
Art: Lindsay Fleming and Silke Lemcke

Omega ProVision Publishing
Printed in the United States of America
ISBN: 978-0-578-41505-5
Library of Congress Control Number: 2018963430

DEDICATION

Ani Adonai Rofecha

. . .

For I am the LORD who heals you.
Exodus 15:26

PREFACE

God gave me a vision wherein authority for healing impacted people's perspective of God, and thereby himself or herself, through anointing authored, living meditations. This collection of healing meditations was birthed out of that vision.

The purpose of each meditation is to encourage faith in God's active plan to heal and restore all things.

As you read, my prayer is that, through engaging The Living God, reflecting on His Word, and exploring each meditation, the Spirit of Truth and Fountain of Faith is stirred within you.

READING SUGGESTION

This text is organized by themes, sections, and meditations. It will serve you best when read in a comfortable, distraction-free environment. Use a journal or notepad to record your experiences, reflections, and thoughts as you make your way through the text. To get the most out of each meditation, read the text once, then pause to reflect on it. Repeat this until you feel ready to move on to the next meditation in the section. Enjoy!

Contents

LIGHT 1

YESHUA 15

LAWFUL 29

ONE 43

NEED 57

SOUND 71

GLORY 85

LIGHT

BIRTHED BY LIGHT

I

Perceived life began
as God spoke light into darkness.
His resounding avowal
opening the eternal narrative.

. . .

Then God said,
"Let there be light";
and there was light.
Genesis 1:3

II

Like the aperture of time
opened by a dawning Word,
I was birthed by light.
At the appointed conception,
light burst in the womb,
my narrative gleamed.

. . .

Thus says the LORD, your Redeemer,
and He who formed you from the womb:
"I am the LORD, who makes all things,
who stretches out the heavens all alone,
who spreads abroad the earth by Myself."
Isaiah 44:24

III

Light is my starting place,
my history and heritage,
my DNA and destiny.
Moving 186,000 miles per second,
in body, soul, and spirit,
in past, present, and future,
light is my legacy.

. . .

And the LORD went before them by day
in a pillar of cloud to lead the way,
and by night in a pillar of fire to give them light,
so as to go by day and night.
Exodus 13:21

THE ANOINTING

I

A light shone in the east,
as a sign of the coming Christ.
Calling to the wise and the working,
light waved glory into night.

. . .

Where is He who has been born King of the Jews?
For we have seen His star in the East
and have come to worship Him.
Matthew 2:2

II

Atop a mountain Christ prayed.
A brilliance of light danced
in the disciple's eyes.
Beyond a shadow of a doubt,
He was transfigured.

. . .

As He prayed, the appearance of His face was altered,
and His robe became white and glistening.
Luke 9:29

III

Christ is the Light of this world.
In the Anointing I have the light of life.
When I live, I am indivisibly light.

. . .

Then Jesus spoke to them again, saying,
"I am the light of the world.
He who follows Me shall not walk in darkness,
but have the light of life."
John 8:12

You are the light of the world.
A city that is set on a hill cannot be hidden.
Matthew 5:14

LIGHT RELEASED

I

The gentle Christ beckons the weary.
His gospel vow is Light,
His burden resplendently weightless.
In His rest, I am radiant.

. . .

For My yoke is easy and
my burden is light.
Matthew 11:30

II

To draw from the well
of my heart's desire,
to become illuminated
I first delight in Christ,
for enlightened faith
dwells within the Word.

. . .

Delight yourself also in the LORD,
and He shall give you the desires of your heart.
Psalm 37:4

III

Across the vault of ages,
loving kindness
surrounds the shining ones
while gracious favor
fulfills the firmament.
The heavens hold wisdom's lights.

. . .

Those who are wise shall shine
like the brightness of the firmament,
and those who turn many to righteousness
like the stars forever and ever.
Daniel 12:3

The LORD make His face shine upon you,
and be gracious to you.
Numbers 6:25

YESHUA

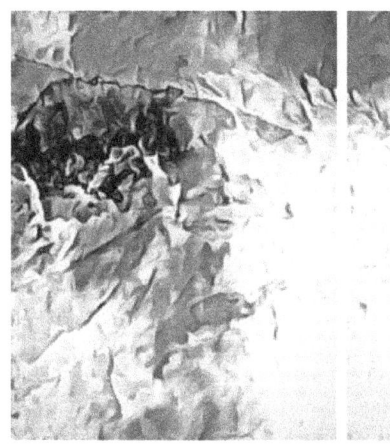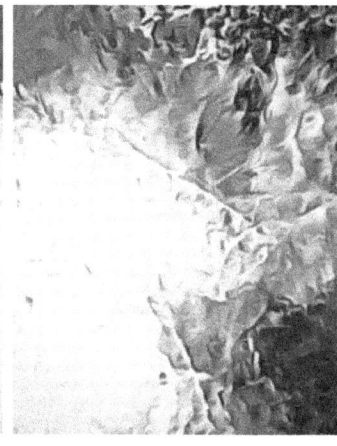

CREATOR

I

Out of the deep,
creation came to light,
its emergence called good.
Ruah, the breath of God,
sealed pleasure
of The Father manifest.

. . .

Then God saw everything that He had made,
and indeed it was very good.
So the evening and the morning were the sixth day.
Genesis 1:31

II

A song encompassing
the sonorous heaven
echoes a single sound,
the Father glorified.
Awesomely alive
in power and peace,
there is only one good.

. . .

*So Jesus said to him,
"Why do you call Me good?
No one is good but One, that is, God."*
Mark 10:18

III

Creation has called You many things.
Now, I call You Indivisible God, All in All,
Consummation of Love, Yeshua.

. . .

And He is before all things,
and in Him all things consist.
Colossians 1:17

THE SLAIN

I

The grave consequence following the fall
pierced creation to cover a covenant failed.
The blood of grace shed for man and woman
clothed their entrance into a broken land.

...

Also for Adam and his wife
the LORD God made tunics of skin,
and clothed them.
Genesis 3:21

II

Since sin and sacrifice creation waits.
Now, suffering soaked land sheds
dry tears from blood-shot eyes
straining to see Salvation complete
as new mercy nourishes a weary life.

. . .

I have waited for your salvation, O LORD!
Genesis 49:18

Therefore the LORD will wait,
that He may be gracious to you;
And therefore He will be exalted,
that He may have mercy on you.
For the LORD is a God of justice;
Blessed are all those who wait for Him.
Isaiah 30:18

III

The horizon promises land's life restored.
An altar, the crowned cross rests
at the gates of the eternal day.
The blood exclaims the fullness of time.

. . .

For the life of the flesh is in the blood,
and I have given it to you upon the altar
to make atonement for your souls;
for it is the blood that makes
atonement for the soul.
Leviticus 17:11

...to Jesus the Mediator of the new covenant,
and to the blood of sprinkling
that speaks better things than that of Abel.
Hebrews 12:24

ARK OF SALVATION

I

The path to receive
the promised land of inheritance,
the healed garden,
is an open wound.
The secret door hedged
in orbiting fire.

. . .

*But he was pierced for our transgressions,
he was crushed for our iniquities;
the punishment that brought us peace was on him,
and by his wounds we are healed.*
Isaiah 53:5

*So He drove out the man; and He placed
cherubim at the east of the garden of Eden,
and a flaming sword which turned every way,
to guard the way to the tree of life.*
Genesis 3:24

II

Unrivaled glory houses creation
in its futility and faith.
The heavens reside in Salvation.

. . .

*You shall make a window for the ark,
and you shall finish it to a cubit from above;
and set the door of the ark in its side.
You shall make it with lower,
second, and third decks.*
Genesis 6:16

III

The pierced lamb's blood,
spotless and silent,
ceased its flow. In rest,
it sought to prepare a place
for forever.

. . .

*But one of the soldiers
pierced His side with a spear,
and immediately
blood and water came out.*
John 19:34

So they departed from the mountain of the LORD on a journey of three days; and the ark of the covenant of the LORD went before them for the three days' journey, to search out a resting place for them.
Numbers 10:33

LAWFUL

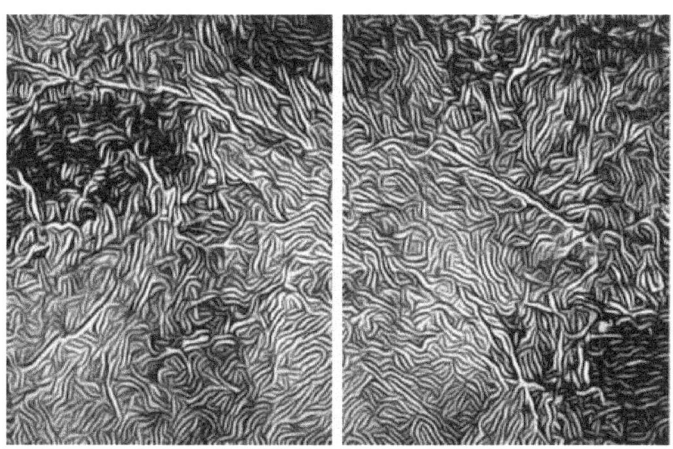

NAMED

I

In his nature, the first man called
creation's covenant character
into place with a name.
What do you call me Lord?

. . .

Out of the ground the LORD God
formed every beast of the field and every bird of the air,
and brought them to Adam
to see what he would call them.
And whatever Adam called each living creature,
that was its name.
Genesis 2:19

But you are a chosen generation,
a royal priesthood, a holy nation, His own special people,
that you may proclaim the praises
of Him who called you out of darkness
into His marvelous light.
1 Peter 2:9

II

Do I know You, whose name is One?
Have I known Your Name?
Do I name You worthy?

...

He said to them,
"But who do you say that I am?"
Simon Peter answered and said,
"You are the Christ,
the Son of the living God."
Matthew 16:15-16

Who is this King of glory?
The LORD strong and mighty,
The LORD mighty in battle.
Psalm 24:8

III

Healing is the guardian
of the city called Peace.
She is the walls and watchmen
waiting for the remnant's return.
Her name is cordial,
her touch the cure.

. . .

...but the Jerusalem above is free,
which is the mother of us all.
Galatians 4:26

He who overcomes, I will make him a pillar
in the temple of My God,
and he shall go out no more.
I will write on him the name of My God
and the name of the city of My God,
the New Jerusalem,
which comes down out of heaven from My God.
And I will write on him My new name.
Revelation 3:12

LINEAGE

I

The birth of sin in the earth
cursed the blood
in the veins of creation
as the death-fruit digested
disseminated its seed.

. . .

The last enemy
that will be destroyed
is death.
1 Corinthians 15:26

II

Take me down, to the place
You created need in me, Rofeh Cholim.
Light the path with mercy and faith.

. . .

He will choose our inheritance for us,
the excellence of Jacob whom He loves.
Psalm 47:4

And my God shall supply
all your need according to His riches
in glory by Christ Jesus.
Philippians 4:19

III

Dust moved on the earth,
as an appearance of God.
The powdered sands and soils
believed into being became
the deponent of destiny.

. . .

He is the image
of the invisible God,
the firstborn over all creation.
Colossians 1:15

And as we have borne the image
of the man of dust,
we shall also bear the image
of the heavenly Man.
1 Corinthians 15:49

TESTAMENT

I

Breath rests within my chest,
an ark encased with flesh,
the space contains a Word
which testifies of Life.

. . .

The Spirit of God has made me,
and the breath of the Almighty gives me life.
Job 33:4

And when He had made an end
of speaking with him on Mount Sinai,
He gave Moses two tablets of the Testimony,
tablets of stone, written with the finger of God.
Exodus 31:18

II

Words inside revolving strands
express dissonant desires while
tongues of fire filter frequency
for one with ears to hear.

. . .

*For with stammering lips
and another tongue
He will speak to this people,
to whom He said,
"This is the rest with which
you may cause the weary to rest,"
and, "This is the refreshing";
Yet they would not hear.*
Isaiah 28:11-12

III

Let every exhale
know my need
as evidence accounted
in the trial of Truth.

. . .

It is also written in your law
that the testimony of two men is true.
I am One who bears witness of Myself,
and the Father who sent Me
bears witness of Me.
John 8:17-18

But the fruit of the Spirit
is love, joy, peace, longsuffering,
kindness, goodness, faithfulness,
gentleness, self-control.
Against such there is no law.
Galatians 5:22-23

ONE

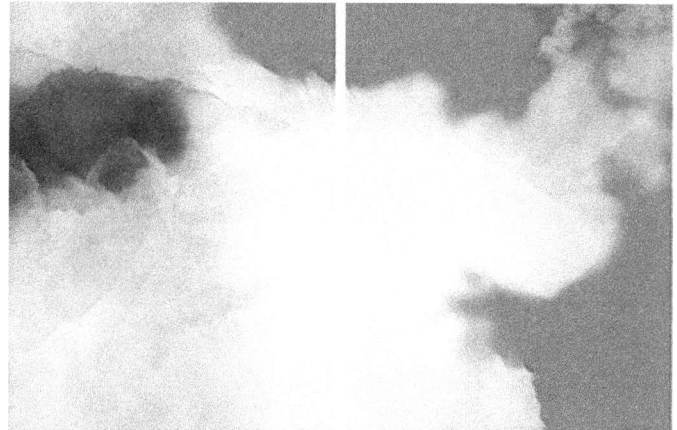

EARTH

I

Believe saints, for the righteousness
of God's chosen land, His Body and Bride.
The fullness of Spirit without measure
in heaven and earth promises
to crucify every cursing cord.

. . .

Where were you
when I laid the foundations of the earth?
Tell Me, if you have understanding.
Job 38:4

For the earnest expectation of the creation
eagerly waits for the revealing of the sons of God.
Romans 8:19

II

Layered coverings
breathe and beckon creation
to don its bridal best.
An iron core residing
beneath the ring aflame,
the greater mantle
drawing all invited in.

. . .

But when the king came in to see the guests,
he saw a man there
who did not have on a wedding garment.
Matthew 22:11

III

Aqueous salvation seeps into the deep, fragrantly flowing frankincense lubricating the channels and corridors of sin-laced wounds. Transfused with grace, the self-afflicted flee from false witness to taste forgiveness.

. . .

So he went to him
and bandaged his wounds,
pouring on oil and wine;
and he set him on his own animal,
brought him to an inn,
and took care of him.
Luke 10:34

And there are three
that bear witness on earth:
the Spirit, the water, and the blood;
and these three agree as one.
1 John 5:8

INDIVISIBLE

I

As I am conformed to the image of Christ,
I wonder what the Father is doing...
So I see the God
of all Power and Peace residing in Rest,
releasing Himself to His remnant.

. . .

Then Jesus answered and said to them,
"Most assuredly, I say to you,
the Son can do nothing of Himself,
but what He sees the Father do;
for whatever He does,
the Son also does in like manner."
John 5:19

II

Becoming transformed,
becoming delivered
is the fruit of the cross.
At Calvary
my healing was sealed.
At resurrection
the Promise of the Father fell sure.

. . .

I in them, and You in Me;
that they may be made perfect in one,
and that the world may know that You have sent Me,
and have loved them as You have loved Me.
John 17:23

III

The clouds are destined
to deliver my Lord
as living witnesses of Glory.
Worthy is He
who rides on the Testimony
of an ash dusted veil torn in two.

. . .

Hear, O Israel:
The Lord our God,
the Lord is one!
Deuteronomy 6:4

REVELATION

I

The present contains
the fullness of time wherein
the Risen One eternally appropriates
His lifeblood perfected,
resurrected in glory.

. . .

All who dwell on the earth will worship him,
whose names have not been written
in the Book of Life of the Lamb
slain from the foundation of the world.
Revelation 13:8

II

He goes before me,
moment by moment,
experiencing every aspect of life.
God is in me, indivisibly intimate
with the totality of natural reality.
Yet deeper still,
Christ suffers and sings
as I do in real time,
for all time, we are one.

. . .

I will go before you and make the crooked places straight;
I will break in pieces the gates of bronze
and cut the bars of iron.
Isaiah 45:2

Then your light shall break forth like the morning,
your healing shall spring forth speedily,
and your righteousness shall go before you;
the glory of the Lord shall be your rear guard.
Isaiah 58:8

III

For His choice
to bear and become the fullness
of suffering for all creation,
the Father faithfully
blesses the Son
with a Kingdom eternal,
perfected through pain
and a love everlasting.

. . .

For You, O Lord, will bless the righteous;
With favor You will surround him as with a shield.
Psalm 5:12

This is the will of the Father who sent Me,
that of all He has given Me I should lose nothing,
but should raise it up at the last day.
John 6:39

NEED

BELIEVE

I

The root of humility
is my need for God.
Since that day in the garden,
how deep have I buried
my singular need,
how gravely do I guard it?

...

*Jesus answered and said to them,
"Those who are well
have no need of a physician,
but those who are sick."*
Luke 5:31

II

The nurses I have known for so very long
are pious pain and the comfort of death.
These counterfeits of life tend to my wounds
with necrotic bandages and carnivorous balms.
And all along, the Healer by bedside waits
until my answer to life is yes,
the death of death.

. . .

When Jesus saw him lying there,
and knew that he already had been
in that condition a long time,
He said to him,
"Do you want to be made well?"
John 5:6

III

The name of my healer is Faith.
Love and Hope, the instruments
for His patient procedures.

...

And He said to her,
"Daughter,
your faith has made you well.
Go in peace,
and be healed of your affliction."
Mark 5:34

SEE

I

God is desperate for His creation
to eat of the Tree of Life again,
to taste the flesh and drink the blood
of the Highest Sacrifice.
Once my body is nourished by Heaven,
my soul will be whole to be and see
the restoration of all things.

. . .

And he looked up and said,
"I see men like trees, walking."
Then He put His hands on his eyes again
and made him look up.
And he was restored
and saw everyone clearly.
Mark 8:24-25

II

See the waves of sound
layered and layering
atoms' fields together
making matter.
As they flow
my sight in Christ
becomes as pure
as the sounds
making up my mind.

. . .

For God has not given us a spirit of fear,
but of power and of love and of a sound mind.
2 Timothy 1:17

III

The first healing, the final healing,
and the cross between them all
rest on their stems in the iris of the present.
As the Husbandman touches the harvest fruit
the delicate morsels nestle into his palms.
I revel in fragrant Truth,
as my faith sees the produce of destiny
plucked from the branches of the vine.

. . .

Beloved, now we are children of God;
And it has not yet been revealed what we shall be,
but we know that when He is revealed,
we shall be like Him, for we shall see Him as He is.
1 John 3:2

See, I have inscribed you on the palms of My hands;
Your walls are continually before Me.
Isaiah 49:16

HEALED

I

One Holy.
All healed.

. . .

And if one member suffers,
all the members suffer with it;
or if one member is honored,
all the members rejoice with it.
1 Corinthians 12:26

II

The Bridegroom
beckons His bride birthed
by blood and water.
In the sound of her sealing vow
is healing culminate.

. . .

And he showed me a pure river of water of life,
clear as crystal, proceeding from the throne of God
and of the Lamb. In the middle of its street,
and on either side of the river, was the tree of life,
which bore twelve fruits, each tree yielding
its fruit every month. The leaves of the tree
were for the healing of the nations.
Revelation 22:1-2

III

The oracle speaks
of the great lights' orbits
reflecting time's lines healing
at the day of completion.

. . .

Moreover the light of the moon
will be as the light of the sun,
and the light of the sun will be sevenfold,
as the light of seven days,
in the day that the Lord
binds up the bruise of His people
and heals the stroke of their wound.
Isaiah 30:26

SOUND

PEACE

I

Your source calls for you
from the gates of life.
She says, "Do you hear?"
"It is my peace to watch and wait,
for your family is here."

. . .

She cries out in the chief concourses,
at the openings of the gates in the city
She speaks her words.
Proverbs 1:21

II

Wisdom's heart pumps blood
through the mercy womb
bearing peace.
As the life grows, the Father
raises the child named Blessed.
Blessed is bestowed a birthright,
betrothal, a ring, and a name.

. . .

And let the peace of God rule in your hearts, to which
also you were called in one body; and be thankful.
Colossians 3:15

Blessed are the peacemakers,
for they shall be called sons of God.
Matthew 5:9

III

Hope blushes with pleasure
at the bliss of her pupils' belief.

. . .

Now may the God of hope
fill you with all joy and peace in believing,
that you may abound in hope
by the power of the Holy Spirit.
Romans 15:13

POWER

I

He waits for one
to carry His word
to term eternal.
His word moves
through the deep
with sonorous resolve.
The polyphonic Patriarch
watches over the womb
as waters break
to deliver it.

. . .

And behold, the glory of the God of Israel
came from the way of the east.
His voice was like the sound of many waters;
And the earth shone with His glory.
Ezekiel 43:2

II

Fertile phrases press upon flesh,
seeding truth in burrows beneath the natural,
beckoning Salvation's Father's fellowship.

. . .

So shall My word be that goes forth from My mouth;
It shall not return to Me void,
but it shall accomplish what I please,
and it shall prosper in the thing for which I sent it.
Isaiah 55:11

III

An iambic lamb abides
in a meadow land
of stars and streets
bestirring infinite intonation.

. . .

Heaven and earth will pass away,
but My words will by no means pass away.
Mark 13:31

PRAYER

I

The law rests as
the advocate sees
the good Judge
of time,
of truth,
of temple.

. . .

For unto us a Child is born,
unto us a Son is given;
And the government will be upon His shoulder.
And His name will be called
Wonderful, Counselor, Mighty God,
Everlasting Father, Prince of Peace.
Isaiah 9:6

II

Oh ancient commandment you call us
to covenant metamorphosis of flesh to fire made
pure by Christ's cries to God.

. . .

As He also says in another place:
"You are a priest forever
According to the order of Melchizedek";
Who, in the days of His flesh,
when He had offered up prayers and supplications,
with vehement cries and tears
to Him who was able to save Him from death,
and was heard because of His godly fear,
though He was a Son,
yet He learned obedience
by the things which He suffered.
Hebrews 5:6-8

III

What substance is man
to the One
whose prayer is Presence?
Cover us as You pass.

. . .

He had in His right hand seven stars, out of His mouth
went a sharp two-edged sword, and His countenance
was like the sun shining in its strength.
Revelation 1:16

GLORY

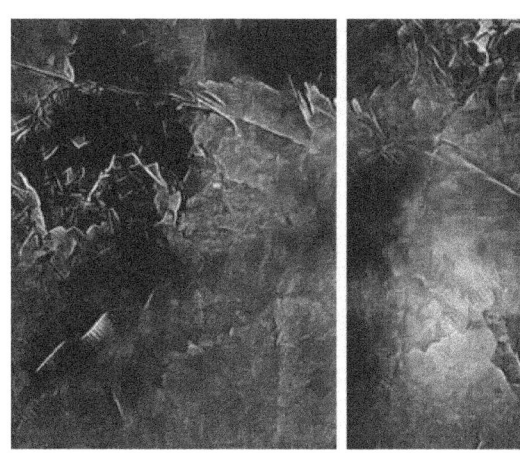

REVEALED

I

The greatest healing happened
in an earthen grave, an opening
sealed by a sphere of rock and ruin.

. . .

Beloved, do not think it strange
concerning the fiery trial which is to try you,
as though some strange thing happened to you;
But rejoice to the extent that you partake
of Christ's sufferings, that when His glory is revealed,
you may also be glad with exceeding joy.
1 Peter 4:12-13

II

Christ walks in sacrifice,
the righteous death
formed by a Father
the fire forsakes no more.
Now Faith is
perfect present
proof in power.

. . .

"Look!" he answered, "I see four men loose, walking in the midst of the fire; and they are not hurt, and the form of the fourth is like the Son of God."
Daniel 3:25

III

Gilded saints healed,
hail the Almighty
when, in time, they find
a Truth revealed eternal.

. . .

But He knows the way that I take;
When He has tested me, I shall come forth as gold.
Job 23:10

GOSPEL

I

Traveling the circumference of God
saints sojourn amidst the to and fro
gospel that sees in every time direction.

. . .

So He drove out the man;
And He placed cherubim at the east
of the garden of Eden,
and a flaming sword which turned every way,
to guard the way to the tree of life.
Genesis 3:24

II

The faces of the gospel
sound like a sWord,
look like a Glory revealed,
smell like an intermingling flame,
and feel like a Kingdom come.

. . .

As for the likeness of their faces,
each had the face of a man;
Each of the four had the face of a lion on the right side,
each of the four had the face of an ox on the left side, and
each of the four had the face of an eagle.
Thus were their faces. Their wings stretched upward;
Two wings of each one touched one another,
and two covered their bodies.
And each one went straight forward;
They went wherever the spirit wanted to go,
and they did not turn when they went.
Ezekiel 1:10-12

III

Christ's love conquered a character complexion
chiding the sons of the earth.
His triumph takes up love's liberty
lavishing His lineage with long suffering.
The culprit confessed is caught.
The belovéd of Christ live.

. . .

They went up on the breadth of the earth and
surrounded the camp of the saints and the beloved city.
And fire came down from God out of heaven and
devoured them. The devil, who deceived them,
was cast into the lake of fire and brimstone
where the beast and the false prophet are.
And they will be tormented
day and night forever and ever.
Revelation 20:9-10

ETERNAL

I

Vision within a Holy chest reveals a heart.
The chambers awaiting the present
swirl with sanguine secrets
of love's eternal life.

. . .

No one has seen God at any time.
The only begotten Son,
who is in the bosom of the Father,
He has declared Him.
John 1:18

II

The fire iris projects the Truth
over the concept of time, hovering
and covering the body parts
revealing the need for resurrection.
In view, inside His side
is the Name of all.

...

His eyes were like a flame of fire,
and on His head were many crowns.
He had a name written
that no one knew except Himself.
Revelation 19:12

III

The composition of Glory found above
breathes creating words that form
a family faithful to the Sovereign's sound,
the Truth's tongue, the Father's face.

. . .

I watched till thrones were put in place,
And the Ancient of Days was seated;
His garment was white as snow,
and the hair of His head was like pure wool.
His throne was a fiery flame,
its wheels a burning fire;
A fiery stream issued
and came forth from before Him.
A thousand thousands ministered to Him;
Ten thousand times ten thousand stood before Him.
The court was seated,
and the books were opened.
Daniel 7:9-10

About the Author

LINDSAY FLEMING has been an imagery explorer since birth and has been writing creatively since grade school. Now, as a seasoned expressionist, inspired writer, and editor she serves to provide clarity, motivation, and coordination. She has been granted an "eye" for the "greater story" and how it is woven throughout the details of individuals, organizations, and communities. Her poetry, blogs, and articles have appeared in a diversity of publications. She currently resides with her husband Matthew and growing family in Charlotte, NC.

More publications are available on Amazon.
Inquiries: thewhisperingpearl@gmail.com

www.ingramcontent.com/pod-product-compliance
Lightning Source LLC
Chambersburg PA
CBHW032332110426
42744CB00036B/234